Captain Kidd's Crew Experiments with Sinking and Floating

by
Mark Weakland

illustrated by
Troy Cummings

PICTURE WINDOW BOOKS
a capstone imprint

Thanks to our advisers for their expertise, research, and advice:
Dr. Paul Ohmann, Associate Professor of Physics, University of St. Thomas
Terry Flaherty, PhD, Professor of English, Minnesota State University, Mankato

Editor: Shelly Lyons
Designer: Lori Bye
Art Director: Nathan Gassman
Production Specialist: Danielle Ceminsky
The illustrations in this book were created digitally.

Picture Window Books
1710 Roe Crest Drive
North Mankato, MN 56003
www.capstonepub.com

Library of Congress Cataloging-in-Publication Data
Weakland, Mark.
 Captain Kidd's crew experiments with sinking and floating / by Mark
Weakland ; illustrated by Troy Cummings.
  p. cm. — (In the science lab)
 Includes index.
ISBN 978-1-4048-7144-1 (library binding)
ISBN 978-1-4048-7236-3 (paperback)
 1. Floating bodies—Juvenile literature. 2. Buoyant ascent
(Hydrodynamics)—Juvenile literature. I. Cummings, Troy, ill. II.
Title.
 QC147.5.W43 2011
 532'.25—dc23
                        2011025843

Printed in the United States of America in North Mankato, Minnesota.
062016   009850R

AHOY, MATE. CAPTAIN KIDD'S ME NAME.
FLOATING AND SINKING IS ME GAME.

PIRATE CAPTAINS HAVE TO KNOW HOW AND WHY BOATS FLOAT
AND ANCHORS SINK. SO COME ABOARD ME SHIP, THE DRIFTWOOD.

Let's start with gravity. Gravity is the force that pulls all objects toward the center of Earth. It's pulling on me, you, the ocean water, and these boats too.

So why doesn't gravity pull *THE DRIFTWOOD* underwater? And why doesn't this rowboat sink like a stone?

gravity

Umm ... 'cause we're held up by invisible sea creatures?

buoyancy

Har, it's not invisible sea creatures! It's buoyancy. Buoyancy is the force of a liquid pushing upward. Gravity and buoyancy work against each other.

Thar she blows!

That's no whale. It's a log floating in the water. Whether something sinks or floats depends upon its density.

Density is the weight of something compared to its size. When an object is denser than the liquid or gas it's in, it sinks. If it's less dense, it floats.

Look out below!

THAT CANNONBALL IS DENSER THAN SEAWATER. WHEN IT HITS THE WATER, IT'LL SINK. BUT THE FEATHER IS LESS DENSE, SO IT FLOATS.

Squawk! That's dense!

BARNACLE BOB'S BOTTLE SHOWS DENSITY. THE CORK IS FULL OF AIR POCKETS. IT HAS LOW DENSITY, SO IT FLOATS. BUT THE GOLD COIN HAS HIGH DENSITY. IT SINKS.

low density

high density

Cap'n, are you tryin' to tell us we're sunk?
THE COIN PUSHED AWAY WATER AS IT SANK. THE CORK ALSO PUSHED AWAY WATER, BUT IT FLOATS. WE PIRATES CALL THIS DISPLACEMENT.
Har, me coin! Never trust a parrot with a cork!

When Crusty sits in the tub, he displaces water. The water's surface rises. The displaced water weighs the same as Crusty.

An object floats if it weighs the same as the water it displaces.

water's surface after Crusty sat down

water's surface before Crusty sat down

THIS IS THE SHIP'S GALLEY.

That's a kitchen! Squawk!

And this is our cook, Grubbs. Grubbs knows that a wooden toothpick floats and a silver spoon sinks.

It seems like light objects

FLOAT

AND HEAVY OBJECTS

SINK.

But heavy ships made of steel float just fine. So why does a giant steel ship float but a small metal spoon sink?

It must have to do with more than an object's weight.

GRUBBS FOLDED ALUMINUM FOIL INTO A LITTLE BOAT. HE ALSO MADE A BALL WITH THE SAME AMOUNT OF FOIL.

THE BOAT IS DENSE, BUT IT'S NOT DENSE ENOUGH TO SINK.

Shiver me timbers, she's floating!

WHAT HAPPENS TO THE FOIL BALL?

It sinks, it sinks!

The weight of the boat and the ball are the same. But the squished ball is much smaller than the boat.

Here's another way to think of it: The tight ball of foil takes up a small amount of space. It has a low volume. It displaces only a small amount of water before it sinks.

ON THE OTHER HAND, THE FOIL BOAT HAS A HIGH VOLUME. IT TAKES UP A LARGE AMOUNT OF SPACE. AND IT CAN DISPLACE A LOT OF WATER TO OFFSET ITS WEIGHT.

AIR POCKETS

That rowboat is made of wood. So is the *Driftwood*. Ocean liners are made of steel. To find the average density of a ship, you must weigh the ship and everything inside it. This includes pockets of air.

Trapped air helps objects float. A heavy steel ship is less dense than the water so it floats. If we pile a ship full of treasure, the ship becomes denser and heavier. There is a smaller amount of air trapped inside it. If it takes on too much treasure, the boat sinks!

Har, there's no such thing as too much treasure!

AIR POCKETS

PIRATES ARE A BIT LIKE SHIPS. POCKETS OF AIR IN OUR LUNGS HELP KEEP US AFLOAT. THE NEXT TIME YOU GO SWIMMING, TAKE A BIG GULP OF AIR. ALL THAT AIR WILL HELP YOU FLOAT. WHILE FLOATING, BREATHE OUT AS MUCH AIR AS YOU CAN. YOU'LL SINK LOWER INTO THE WATER.

AIR

OL' PEG LEG IS LOADED DOWN WITH SWORDS AND PISTOLS AND JEWELS. HE'LL PROBABLY SINK LIKE A STONE.

He's too dense, **squawk!**

But if he were wearing a life preserver, Peg Leg's density would be less. And his buoyancy would increase. Once he gets that preserver on, Peg Leg will float like a boat.

Density, volume, and the forces of buoyancy and gravity combine in many ways. Different combinations mean some objects float and others sink. Cannonballs sink. So does the dense ball of foil. Feathers and corks float. So does me trusty *Driftwood*.

I'M GLAD ME CREW AND I ARE FLOATERS, NOT SINKERS. FOR THERE'S NOTHING I'D RATHER BE THAN A PIRATE CAPTAIN FLOATING ON A SALTY SEA!

GLOSSARY

buoyancy—the upward force of a liquid on an object

density—the weight of something compared to its size

displacement—the weight or volume of the water an object pushes away

force—any action that changes the movement of an object

gravity—a force that pulls objects together; gravity pulls objects toward the center of Earth

volume—the amount of space taken up by an object

TO LEARN MORE

More Books to Read

Boothroyd, Jennifer. *What Floats? What Sinks?: A Look at Density*. Exploring Physical Science. Minneapolis: Lerner Publications, 2011.

Guillain, Charlotte. *Floating or Sinking*. Properties of Materials. Chicago: Heinemann Library, 2009.

Hansen, Amy. *Floating and Sinking*. My Science Library. Vero Beach, Fla.: Rourke Pub., 2012.

Internet Sites

FactHound offers a safe, fun way to find Internet sites related to this book. All of the sites on FactHound have been researched by our staff.

Here's all you do:

Visit www.facthound.com

Type in this code: 9781404871441

Super-cool stuff! Check out projects, games and lots more at www.capstonekids.com

23

Index

Look For All the Books in the Series:

Captain Kidd's Crew Experiments with

Sinking and Floating

DO-4U the Robot Experiences

Forces and Motion

Gertrude and Reginald the Monsters Talk about

Living and Nonliving

Joe-Joe the Wizard Brews Up

Solids, Liquids, and Gases